THE

Longest

TABLE

52 MEDITATIONS
for COMMUNION

J. LEE MAGNESS

Standard®
PUBLISHING
Bringing The Word to Life

Cincinnati, Ohio

Published by Standard Publishing, Cincinnati, Ohio
www.standardpub.com
Copyright © 2007 by Lee Magness

Interior design: Edward Willis Group, Inc.

07 08 09 10 11 12   9 8 7 6 5 4 3 2 1

TABLE OF CONTENTS

The Longest Table, *Maryland*..5

All the Blood Is His, *Mexico* 7

All the Broken Pieces, *Czech Republic*............................9

Another Upper Room, *Tennessee* 11

At His Footstool Kneeling, *Iceland*..............................13

Binding the Broken, *California* 15

The Bloody Crucifix, *West Virginia* 17

Bringing in the Cross, *China* 19

Christmas Needs Communion, *China*............................21

Digging His Grave, *Mexico* 23

Dirty Feet, *Egypt*...25

Drawing in the Dust, *Iran*.....................................27

The Emperor's Table, *Austria* 29

Encountering Christ, *Japan* 31

Everyone Is Equal, *China* 33

Father, Forgive, *Great Britain* 35

The Feast of Regeneration, *Russia*............................37

First Meal, Last Meal, *China* 39

The First Meal on the Moon, *The Moon* 41

First Thanksgiving, *Massachusetts*............................43

Grain and Grapes, *Czech Republic* 45

Greeting the Rising Son, *Iceland* 47

Hanging on a Tree, *Germany* 49

He Broke It, *Japan*...51

Her Own Share, *China* 53

In Our Gladness, *Russia* 55

In the Presence of His Enemies, *Turkey* 57

Judas' Eyes, Jesus' Eyes, *Singapore*...........................59

The King of the Hawaiians, *Hawaii*.............................61

Marching with the Cross, *Korea*................................63

Michelangelo's Masterpiece, *Italy*.............................65

A Monsoon Meal, *India*...67

A Monument to Love, *India* 69

Naked at the Cross, *China* 71

Not Just Words, *Australia*.....................................73

A Part of the Whole, *India*....................................75

A Place of Peace, *Great Britain* 77

The Saddest Place in the World, *Ghana* 79

The Shepherd Wears a Crown, *Tennessee*.........................81

Slave to the Slaves, *Colombia* 83

Something's Fishy, *Germany* 85

Speaking His Language, *Greece* 87

Standing Up Together, *Georgia* 89

Strapped to the Cross, *Pennsylvania* 91

They Still Ate, *Japan* 93

Thunder at the River, *China*...................................95

Tokens of Triumph, *Great Britain*..............................97

Traveling by Starlight, *Turkey*................................99

Unbinding Their Feet, *China* 101

With all the Saints, *Spain* 103

With What We Have, *France* 105

Zero Degrees Longitude, *Great Britain* 107

Scripture Index 109

Topical Index 110

THE LONGEST TABLE

When the hour came, Jesus and his apostles reclined at the table. (Luke 22:14)

The longest table I had ever seen was my grandmother's Thanksgiving dinner table. It stretched through the living room of her farmhouse and across the dining room. It was so long that there was a place for all her children and grandchildren and great-grandchildren. It was so long that there was room for folks far from home, visitors from Germany, from Japan. It was so long that there was a place for the elderly, broken man who had been Grandmother's first husband. And it was so long that it was never quite full until absent family members were brought back, either by fond remembrance or by an everyone-talk-at-once phone call. It was Thanksgiving at Grandmother's house, and it was the longest table I had ever seen.

But I came to know better. I came to know that this table is the longest table in the world. It too is a Thanksgiving table, and I know now just how far it stretches. I have sat at this table in many states of the Union and many countries of Europe, in Thailand and Turkey, in India and Israel, in Egypt and China and Papua New Guinea. It is so long that there is room for the well-to-do in Westminster Abbey, for the workaday women of Athens, for peasant farmers in India. And in each of those places there was room for me. There is always room for the repentant, relatives in Christ who haven't always acted like they were related to us or to him. And this table is never quite full until we have recalled to our minds all those we have sipped with and supped with, now far from home, but never far from this longest table.

So today we think not only of our Lord. We think also of the guests, those we see and those we can't quite see but remember, sitting just around the corner in Grandmother's dining room, just over the curve of the earth, at this longest table.

God, help us to remember just how long this table is, this table at which you long to have us sit, through Jesus, Amen.

THE BLOOD IS HIS

Day after day every priest stands and performs
his religious duties; again and again he offers the same
sacrifices, which can never take away sins. But when
this priest had offered for all time one sacrifice for sins,
he sat down at the right hand of God . . . because by one
sacrifice he has made perfect forever those who are
being made holy. (Hebrews 10:11, 12, 14)

On a rocky plateau in the Yucatan peninsula lies an
ancient city that drew people with the power of a magnet.
It still does. The place is Chichen Itza. This magnificent
Mayan city was the center of a great civilization, a center
for social and cultural gatherings, for civic activities,
athletic competitions, and scientific investigations, all in
the context of religious observance.

But Chichen Itza was also a bloody place—not the
blood of foreign invasion or intertribal warfare, but of
human sacrifice. This part of Mayan religion touched every
activity, every aspect of their lives. Even the famous ball
games of the Mayans—striking balls through stone rings
mounted high up on stone walls, without the use of hands
or feet—ended in human sacrifice. The only question is
whether it was the loser or the winner who was sacrificed.

The temple in Jerusalem was also a bloody place.
Priests slaughtered animals and laid them on the altar

as sacrifices to God. But there was one sacrifice that ended all other sacrifices, the sacrifice of the high priest himself. Even now some people call the Lord's table an altar, reminding us of the inescapable connection between communion and sacrifice.

We come dragging no lamb or goat, only ourselves, remembering Jesus who died not as the loser but as the victor. And we recognize in his sacrifice the sacrifice that ended the other sacrifices. But just as surely as the sacrifice of Jesus ended animal sacrifices, so his sacrifice was the beginning of sacrifices, the living sacrifices that are our lives. This is a bloody place we come to today. But all the blood is his.

O God, we thank you for that final, sufficient sacrifice, for Jesus our high priest. Now we ask that you accept the sacrifice of our lives, through Jesus, Amen.

ALL THE BROKEN PIECES

While they were eating, Jesus took bread, gave thanks and broke it, and gave it to his disciples, saying, "Take and eat; this is my body." (Matthew 26:26)

The horrors that a Czech poet observed in the final dark days of World War II remind us, sadly but significantly, of the Lord's Supper. He recalls seeing children standing outside a candy shop in Charles Square: "They were pale,/they borrowed shoes from each other and breathed/on the tips of fingers without nails."* We come to this table much like those children—weak and weary. We come, while we were yet sinners. We come on borrowed time, on borrowed mercy. We stand in need—some of us cold, some barely breathing, some spiritually starving.

The poet tells how the children stood in line, "patiently, humbly, grateful in advance" for some cotton candy, "that sweet air, because there was nothing else for sale." We come to this table expecting something sweet in the otherwise bitter circumstances of our lives. It doesn't seem like much—"sweet air"— but it is enough, so we gather here "patiently, humbly, grateful in advance," knowing that there is "nothing else" that saves. Then the poet describes "a hungry boy running with a briefcase," running to get communion wafers at the baker's, "looking forward/to eating all the broken pieces." We come to this table hungry, running on empty, eager to fill our mouths, our lives, with Communion, eager to eat all the broken pieces. We come humbly but hungrily, eager to stuff ourselves on these bread bits of his body, these crumbs of Christ, the leftovers of our Lord. We come as all his broken people come, hungry for all the broken pieces that he blessed and broke and gave. The bread tastes bitter like blood, stale as a nail. But we eat anyway, convinced that we will get a little something like grace, in the midst of our pathetic wars and our petty peaces, standing bare-toed and bare-fingered before the One who now invites us to the table.

God, for all the broken pieces we give you thanks, and entrust ourselves to you, all us broken people, in the name of the Broken One, Amen.

Vladimir Holan, "Children at Christmas in 1945," Mirroring *(Middletown, Connecticut: Wesleyan University Press 1985).*

ANOTHER UPPER ROOM

He will show you a large room upstairs, furnished and ready. Make preparations for us there. (Mark 14:15)

It was an upper room. He gathered with friends after a journey. There was quite a demonstration when he arrived. Victory was on their lips, but it left a bad taste in his mouth. He had spoken to hopeful crowds, fringed with suspicious officials. Now he rested in the upper room, reminding them of his principles—do not resist your enemy, turn the other cheek. This April evening he sounded almost pessimistic, speaking of his own mortality. Eventually he got hungry and called for food to be brought up. Only one plate arrived, his favorite food for what would be his last supper—catfish. An associate complained that there wouldn't be enough for all of them. He laid the plate down on the bed and said, "All of you, have some." Then Martin Luther King, Jr. stepped out onto the balcony of the upper room, Room 306 of the Lorraine Motel in Memphis, Tennessee. The rest, as they say, is history.

It was an upper room. He gathered there with disciples after a journey. There was quite a demonstration when he arrived. Triumph was on their lips, but it left a bad taste in his mouth. He had spoken to hopeful crowds, fringed with suspicious officials. Now he rested in the upper room, reminding them of his principles—serve one another, humble yourselves. This April evening he sounded almost pessimistic, speaking again of his own death. Eventually the festival food was served, simple food for what would be his last supper—unleavened bread and Passover wine. He said, "Eat, drink, all of you." Then Jesus stepped out into the spring night, into the garden of Gethsemane. The rest, we might say, is memory.

Here we are, gathered with our Lord. Our stomachs are beginning to grumble. And the one who invited us to the table today has said, amazingly enough, "All of you, have some." The rest, we might say, is mystery.

God, help us to speak clearly of his death on the day of his resurrection, and help us to celebrate his life by the commemoration of his death, through Jesus, Amen.

AT HIS FOOTSTOOL KNEELING

Since, then, we have a great high priest who has
passed through the heavens, Jesus, the Son of God,
let us hold fast to our confession. . . . Let us therefore
approach the throne of grace with boldness,
so that we may receive mercy and find grace
to help in time of need. (Hebrews 4.14, 16)

Hallgrimur Petursson, the great priest-poet of Iceland, published a series of poetic meditations on the Passion of Christ in the year 1666. Starting with the agony of Jesus in the garden of Gethsemane and following Jesus to the cross and to his victorious resurrection, Petursson explored the paradoxes and the power of Jesus' suffering and sacrificial death. In his reflection on the betrayal and arrest of Jesus, Petursson thinks of himself and his readers gathered at the Lord's Supper. He writes,

When thou by faith partakest
Of his memorial feast,
Pause, ere thy way thou makest
To meet thy great High Priest.
Look to each inward feeling,
Give him no thoughtless kiss,
Low at his footstool kneeling,
Thy heart prepare for this.*

Petursson reminds us that when we gather at this meal, we must do so faithfully not forgetfully, focused primarily on the person, our Priest, even more than on the setting or the symbols or the fellow sinners with whom we gather. The poet asks that we gather thoughtfully not thoughtlessly, lest we too betray our Lord. He challenges us to examine our inmost thoughts and feelings, not to condemn or disqualify ourselves but to stay our hearts on Jesus. He calls on us to come prepared, spiritually and emotionally and mentally prepared for this encounter with Jesus. And finally this powerful piece of Christian poetry challenges us to come to the table humbly, kneeling at this table as if it were a throne.

Help us to come, O God, to partake of this memorial feast, fully prepared and fully focused on our great high Priest, in his name, Amen.

---

* *Hallgrimur Petursson,* Hymns of the Passion *VI.9 (Reykjavik: Hallgrims Church, 1978).*

BINDING THE BROKEN

The Spirit of the Lord God is upon me, because the Lord has anointed me; he has sent me to bring good news to the oppressed, to bind up the brokenhearted. (Isaiah 61:1)

In one of the moving moments of Cecil B. de Mille's 1927 silent classic, *King of Kings*, Jesus welcomes a group of playful children. Cameras record the children playing among the fruit trees in the director's own back yard in southern California. When Jesus arrives, they flock, like sheep to a shepherd, to his side in typical, let-the-little-children-come-unto-me fashion. Judas tries to keep them from clamoring around him. But the cinematic Jesus sits down with children all around, one tucked under each arm, their finally glad faces fixed on his.

Then the filmmaker adds an interesting touch. One little girl holds up her wooden doll with moveable legs. One leg has broken off. Can you fix it? her sad eyes say from the silent screen. Jesus takes the doll and the leg. He looks at a loss, fumbling a bit, fitting the leg into the socket only to have it fall free again. But then he takes a twig, sticks it through the pivot holes, and hands the doll back to the little girl, dangling legs and all, whole again.

That is the message of this table. Jesus heals what is broken, not just the broken-bodied, but the brokenhearted, not just broken people but broken relationships, not just with the children of God but with God. The mender is not only the binder of bodies and relationships but of all things broken, of this whole broken world. Jesus binds the broken by being broken, all broken, for us, us all, broken.

He did it by his own loss, taking a stick no bigger than a cross, and sticking it into the pivot holes of the whole hurting world, allowing himself to be broken upon it. Then he handed back to us all that had been broken, our very lives. He broke the bread and said, "This is my body broken for you."

God, thank you for the one who was broken for our sakes. Help us to be willing to offer our brokenness to him, in his name, Amen.

THE BLOODY CRUCIFIX

But he was pierced for our transgressions,
he was crushed for our iniquities; the punishment
that brought us peace was upon him,
and by his wounds we are healed. (Isaiah 53:5)

You might expect to see something like it in a cathedral in Europe, but not in a quaint church, not on a trail, not in West Virginia—the bloodiest crucifix you are ever likely to see.

Just after the Appalachian Trail crosses the Potomac River, passing the old armory where John Brown staged his infamous raid, in the town of Harper's Ferry, well-worn stone steps climb the steep hill to a little church. Just inside the door and to the right, in a poorly lit alcove, hangs the bloody crucifix—a Christ-on-the-cross ripped by the razor-sharp stones studding the scourge with which they had whipped his weary body.

Some can stand the sight only a few seconds, others stare with the stare of one ensnared by the too-grotesque. Many who stand there on the edge of the darkness find their eyes drawn away from the bloody streaks stretching from face to foot, to the ragged, repulsive, cut-to-the-bone knee.

You think of other crucifixes you have seen, with a trickle of blood here and there, of bloodless, bodiless crosses. You wonder what a body beaten by glass-tipped thongs would look like, if not this. What a knee knocked repeatedly to the rocky road under the weight of a wooden cross would look like, if not this. Would it be an accurate representation of the cross if it did not drive away or draw our eyes in revulsion?

"He was despised and rejected by men: . . . Like one from whom men hide their faces he was despised" (Isaiah 53:3).

The bloody crucifix reminds us that we believe in a Christ not only glorified but crucified. And this meal has the same effect. We eat—this is his lacerated body—and we drink—this cup is the new covenant in his shed blood—for the same reason we stare at that bloody crucifix—so that from now on we won't forget either.

God, we pray that you help us glory in nothing if not in the cross, through the crucified One, Amen.

BRINGING IN THE CROSS

"But I, when I am lifted up from the earth,
will draw all men to myself." (John 12:32)

A faithful Chinese Christian writes this story: "The cross has been the centre of our lives and of our meetings. This wooden cross, hand-carved for us by a kind young man, is our fifth. We always begin our meetings, as in the old days, with the cross coming into our midst.

"The first was silver, my family's cross. It came in very useful when, towards the end of the fifties, Pastor Pi lost his church and asked my husband if he and others could use our home for prayers. With him the cross was always the centre. At some time during this period, the silver cross was stolen. I was able to locate another cross, an ivory one. We met around the ivory cross.

"Then the Cultural Revolution came upon us. One day, my neighbour's 14-15 year-old son . . . quietly tipped me off about 'a house confiscation' visit by the Red Guards any time. My husband . . . told me to get rid of the ivory cross. So I hid it in the charcoal pile in the kitchen. Three days later they arrived. They found my ivory cross with ease. The leader took it right in front of me, moved his young head in mock pity, let the cross fall and crushed it with his foot.

"Then I decided to make a small cross for myself.

I carried it all the time in my pocket, touching it and remembering Jesus.

"Now we've got a bigger cross, hand carved by one of our young people. We let him bring in the cross."*

These words from a faithful Chinese Christian remind us that the cross must always be at the center of our lives as well. She reminds us that, in breaking this bread and drinking this cup, we "bring in the cross," "showing forth his death until he comes again." She reminds us that to touch the cross means to remember Jesus.

God, as we come to this meal, help us to understand our eating and drinking as a way of "bringing in the cross," through Jesus, Amen.

Raymond Fung, ed., Households of God on China's Soil *(Maryknoll, NY: Orbis Books, 1983).*

CHRISTMAS NEEDS COMMUNION

"This child is destined to cause the falling and rising of many in Israel, . . . a sign that will be spoken against . . . and a sword will pierce your own soul too." (Luke 2:34, 35)

Why celebrate Communion at Christmas? Why mar the marvel of his birth with the memory of his death?

During China's Cultural Revolution, Christians were often sentenced to hard labor in prison camps. Maintaining their faith was hard; expressing it was harder. But for one man, Christmas was not complete without Communion. The significance of Jesus' birth and death made celebrating Communion on a cold Christmas Day worth the risk.

Christmas 1961 found the prisoners outside in zero degree temperatures, working on earthen walls around rice paddies. Wind howled over the frozen ground. One prisoner, crouching in the cold, approached his supervisor. Could he have some time off from work, since it was such a special day? What special day? Christmas. The guard gave him permission, warning him to beware the warden. The old man climbed down into a gully, out of sight, out of the wind. He built a small fire and began to celebrate Christmas. A few minutes later the friendly guard saw a warden headed straight for them. He hurried over to warn the old prisoner, just in time to see him standing in his often ripped, often repaired work clothes, sipping something from a chipped cup, eating a bite of bread. When the warden arrived, all he saw were a prisoner and a guard huddled by a small fire. But the prisoner had completed his Christmas celebration, not with a banquet or with sweets but with a cold cup and a cold crust—with Communion. His celebration of Christmas demanded communion.

The birth of Jesus would leave us cold, if not for the death of Jesus, enfolding us in the warm glow of his mercy. Our celebration of his bare birth needs to be wrapped in the swaddling clothes of God's grace. Our awe at advent is not that he came at all, but that he came to be crucified.

God, we gather at the cradle and at the cross, remembering Jesus, born for us, dying for us, risen for us. We pray in his name, Amen.

DIGGING HIS GRAVE

God made him who had no sin to be sin for us,
so that in him we might become the
righteousness of God. (2 Corinthians 5:21)

Nobel Prize winning novelist, Kenzaburo Oe ("o-ay"),
tells this story of a Japanese woman in *An Echo of Heaven*.
She had suffered a series of tragedies, including the
traumatic deaths of her two sons. Searching for meaning
in a meaningless life, she migrated to Mexico. There she
lived among poverty-stricken peasants on a cooperative
farm, working with them in the fields, encouraging the
depressed, and tending the sick. She salved her own sores
by ministering to those more miserable than she.

One night a *mestizo* raped her. Days later he raped her
again. Each time she refused to bring charges against him,
continuing her ministry in the close-knit community. But
the villagers knew. One night they way-laid the wayward
man and smashed his kneecaps, leaving him crippled for life.

Eventually the woman contracted cancer, suffered
while still serving, and died, in pain but at peace. News of
her death spread quickly throughout the village. While the
villagers stood paralyzed by their sudden grief, someone
noticed a crippled man awkwardly, painfully, lock-kneed,
digging her grave with a crude mattock under the merciless
Mexican sun. It was a silent symbol of repentance. It was

an act of grace from one who had confronted grace in the violating of it.

Jesus came to share our lives, to labor alongside us, to challenge, encourage, and heal us. He shared our suffering and the consequences of our sin. In response we rejected him, refused the grace of his life. We betrayed him, arrested him, condemned him, mocked him, pierced him, and killed him. Shamefully we put him to shame. Through it all, he Father-forgave us.

This table is the silent symbol of our repentance. It is an act of grace in which we, crippled, guilty as we are, confront the very grace we have violated. By remembering his death, we dig his grave, as it were. But it is a grave from which he arose to give us life.

God, forgive us our sin which resulted in the death of Jesus, and thank you for the death of Jesus which rescued us from our sin, through Jesus, Amen.

DIRTY FEET

Jesus . . . got up from the meal, took off his outer
clothing, and wrapped a towel around his waist.
After that, he poured water into a basin and began
to wash the disciples' feet, drying them with the towel
that was wrapped around him. (John 13:3-5)

Origen, one of our greatest Christian teachers, lived in
Alexandria, Egypt, during the third century AD Reflecting
on the story of Jesus washing the feet of his incredulous
disciples, Origen prayed this prayer of repentance: "O
Jesus, my feet are dirty. Come even as a slave to me, pour
water into your bowl, come and wash my feet."*

Repentance is a lost art—in conversion, in worship, and
in prayer. Why? Perhaps because we don't take our own sin
seriously.

Our conversion must include not only faith (our
confession of Christ) and baptism (our commitment to
Christ) but also repentance—reorienting ourselves toward
Christ. Our worship must include not only praise for God's
greatness, and thanks for his gifts, and remembrance of his
grace, but also repentance, admitting our alienation. Our
prayer must include not only praise for what God has done
and petition for what he might yet do, but also repentance
for the times we care too much—anxiety—and the times we
care too little—insensitivity.

When Origen thought about repentance, he thought about the Upper Room. And so should we. It is here, at this table, that our arrogance is washed away in the basin of his humility. It is here that our temptation to don't-know-him denial is confronted by his feed-my-sheep forgiveness. It is here that our penchant for power is subverted by his servitude. It is here that our quest for self-protection is called into question by his self-sacrifice. It is here, at this table, that we say most meaningfully, "O Jesus, our feet are dirty. Come even as a slave to us, pour water into your bowl, come and wash our feet."* It is here that we repent.

God, we know all too well why we must repent. Now give us the will to do it. Come and wash our feet, we pray, through Jesus, Amen.

---

*Desmond Tutu, ed., An African Prayer Book *(New York: Doubleday, 1995).*

DRAWING IN THE DUST

"Then neither do I condemn you," Jesus declared.
"Go now and leave your life of sin." (John 8:11)

The artist who painted "Jesus with the Woman
Taken in Adultery" knew what it meant to be an outcast.
Hossein Behzad, famous Iranian painter of miniatures,
had struggled with drug addiction and alcoholism in his
youth. When he converted to Christianity, he escaped his
addictions but quickly found himself facing discrimination
from his Muslim culture. Hossein Behzad knew what it
meant to be an outcast.

His visual depiction of the gospel scene of the woman
taken in adultery shows Jesus sitting on the ground,
leaning on one hand, his head bent thoughtfully, drawing
in the dust. The bejeweled woman, her long black hair
cascading uncovered down her back, arms demurely folded
across her chest, watches intently as Jesus inscribes the
Iranian dirt. In the background of the painting turbaned
men retreat from the seated pair, the stinging words of
Jesus ringing in their ears. But the unique feature of
Behzad's exquisite painting is what he has Jesus drawing
in the dirt. The gospel of John gives us no clue. One
popular guess has been that Jesus was scratching the sins
of the accusing, now accused, onlookers. Some interpreters
assume Jesus was just doodling while he waited for the

situation to sink in, to the woman and to her accusers. But Behzad shows Jesus drawing a cross, a cross, in the dirt, a foreshadowing of the sacrifice by which he would forgive all of us, just as he had that woman, that outcast.

We come to this table outcasts ourselves. But at this table we have the opportunity to draw in the dirt, as it were, to make an impression, to carve the cross into each of our minds. This bread and this cup remind us of the cross and of the sacrifice by which he has forgiven all of us outcasts. It is here that we encounter the merciful words of Jesus, "Neither do I condemn you." And it is here that we encounter the call of Christ to "go and sin no more."

God, thank you for Jesus and for the cross. Engrave it deeply in our hearts and forgive us, through Jesus, Amen.

THE EMPEROR'S TABLE

*So he got up from the meal, took off his outer clothing,
and wrapped a towel around his waist. After that,
he poured water into a basin and began to wash
his disciples' feet, drying them with the towel
that was wrapped around him.* (John 13:4, 5)

Every Good Friday, Franz Joseph, Emperor of the
Austro-Hungarian Empire, and his wife Elisabeth invited
twelve subjects to the royal apartments of the Hofburg
Palace. They must be old, and they must be poor. First they
had a sumptuous meal with the fabulously wealthy but pious
rulers. Then a wooden tub was brought out. The Emperor
and Empress washed the feet of the least of their people,
pouring water over their feet with a pitcher and bowl used
for royal baptisms. After the foot washing they gave gifts,
including a container of wine and thirty pieces of silver.

There are some interesting parallels between this Good
Friday custom and the Last Supper. Jesus invited twelve
people to a Passover meal. They were commoners, neither
noteworthy nor noble, and poor after following Jesus for
three years—"the least of these my brethren." Jesus also
used the occasion of hosting a grand meal to humbly wash
the feet of his guests—the Sovereign acting the part of the
Servant. And just as Franz Joseph and Elisabeth gave gifts
of thirty coins, the price of Judas' betrayal, so Jesus used

the Last Supper to predict not only Judas' betrayal but also the denial of Peter and the flight of his fellow disciples.

There are also some interesting parallels between the imperial Austrian custom and what we do at this table. Most of us come as commoners, spiritually poor if not financially poor. We come to a meal—not a banquet, but spiritually sumptuous nonetheless. We come aware of the humility of our crucified King, resolved to keep the basin and towel close to our table. And we try to keep a conscious connection between our baptism and our communions. Most of all we come to this table aware of the gift we have been given—our Sovereign is also our Savior.

Thanks be to you, O God, for your inexpressible gift, through Jesus, who is that gift, Amen.

ENCOUNTERING CHRIST

When he was at table with them, he took bread, broke it and began to give it to them. Then their eyes were opened and they recognized him, and he disappeared from their sight.... They got up and returned at once to Jerusalem. There they found the Eleven and those with them, assembled together.... Then the two told what had happened on the way, and how Jesus was recognized by them when he broke the bread. (Luke 24:30, 31, 33, 35)

The mother of Rinzo Shiina attempted suicide days after his birth. At seven his parents separated. At fourteen his impoverished mother and disinterested father turned him out. He worked on the railroad, joining a Labor Union. In 1933 he was arrested for being a Communist. In prison he recanted his communism, was released, and went on to become one of Japan's most famous writers.

The Christian authors he had read in prison continued to influence him and in 1950 he was baptized into Christ. He was a little disappointed that "nothing happened." He still struggled with the same miseries, the same fears. Then one day while reading the story of Jesus' encounter with the two on the road to Emmaus, something did happen. When he read about Jesus breaking the bread, it was as if he too recognized the risen Christ. "I could almost see Christ showing his hairy legs and earnestly holding out both his hands. It seemed ludicrous! And yet at the next instant I, this balding old man, felt something strike me through to my very heart."

The world of two men from ancient Palestine and the world of one man from modern Japan were shaken to their foundations by the recognition of the risen Lord in the breaking of the bread. At this table, we too are looking at evidences of his death, coming face to face as it were with "Christ showing his hairy legs and earnestly holding out both his hands." At this table we encounter Christ, in these very crumbs and this very cup.

God, we thank you for the recognition of the Risen Christ in these emblems of his death, for an encounter with our Savior, in whose name we pray, Amen.

EVERYONE IS EQUAL

Jesus said to them, "The kings of the Gentiles lord it over them; and those who exercise authority over them call themselves Benefactors. But you are not to be like that. Instead, the greatest among you should be like the youngest, and the one who rules like the one who serves. For who is greater, the one who is at the table or the one who serves? Is it not the one who is at the table? But I am among you as one who serves. (Luke 22:25-27)

A Chinese Christian elder describes the impact of the Lord's Supper on Christian worship and on Christian life. He writes, "A long while ago, we made a decision to be a holy people, setting ourselves apart for the cause of the gospel. I have been made the Responsible Brother for a period of three years. I pray, I study the scriptures, I examine the faith of the believers. At the service, I cease to be the Responsible Brother. Before the direct presence of God everyone is equal. Every worship service is a communion service: Christ speaking to his disciples. Any one of us can break bread."*

Our brother reminds us that "every worship service is a communion service." The heart of our worship is this meal. He reminds us that at the table "Christ is speaking." Our Communion involves listening to the Lord who saves. And he reminds us that at this table, "everyone is equal." In coming we are equally famished. In leaving we are equally filled. We all serve, and we are all served.

He reminds us not only of the centrality of Christ at this table but also of the humility of Christ with which we approach this table. We come with the mind of Christ, not lording it over one another, as we would like to do. We come in the manner of our Lord, sitting at the table as one who serves, as he would like us to do.

God, we empty our eyes of all but the cross and we grasp the hands of the brother and sister with whom you have graced us, through Jesus, Amen.

Raymond Fung, ed., Households of God on China's Soil *(Maryknoll, NY: Orbis Books, 1983).*

FATHER, FORGIVE

Jesus said, "Father, forgive them, for they
do not know what they are doing." (Luke 23:34)

A thousand years ago, Magnus of Scotland was
earl over half the Orkney Islands. He ruled his people
kindly, fostering a deep devotion to God in his own life
and encouraging faith among his subjects. He harbored
no sense of rivalry with his co-ruler. His subjects loved
him and later islanders revered him, not so much for his
miracles as for the manner of his life and death.

Although Magnus was content with sharing rule of
the islands, his fellow earl was not. The rival continually
prodded his soldiers into armed conflict with Magnus'
supporters. When this war-like earl suggested a peace
conference to discuss the deteriorating political climate,
Magnus eagerly agreed. The rules were clear: the meeting
would be peaceful, and no one would be armed. But the
envious earl had brought armed warriors and seized the
unprotected Magnus. Magnus offered to relinquish his
earldom in exchange for his life. But the rival realized that
as long as Magnus lived the people would look to him as
their legitimate leader. When the soldiers refused to slay
this godly man, the earl ordered a cowering cook to commit
the assassination. Magnus looked compassionately on the
terrified cook and promised him his and God's forgiveness.

Magnus bent before his executioner, the cook raised a shaking meat cleaver, and it split Magnus' skull.

We too gather at this table to remember the manner of his life and death. We remember him as our kindly and crucified king. We remember how he bowed before his enemies. And we gather here all too painfully aware of the fact that it was in a sense, a very real sense, we who put him to death. But the story of Magnus of Scotland demands that we also remember that we who are guilty of his death have already been forgiven of it, and of every other sin we have committed or will commit.

Thank you, God, for your Son, who yielded to the effects of our sin even as he overcame them. Help us to forgive, even as we have been forgiven, through Jesus, Amen.

THE FEAST OF REGENERATION

See! The winter is past; the rains are over and gone. Flowers appear on the earth; the season of singing has come, the cooing of doves is heard in our land. The fig tree forms its early fruit; the blossoming vines spread their fragrance. (Song of Songs 2:11-13)

Over 800 years ago, Cyril preached a beautiful and meaningful sermon on the resurrection. Spring had finally come to the cold Russian steppes. But he could not think about spring without thinking of the resurrection. And he could not think about the resurrection without thinking of what he called the "feast of regeneration." Cyril wrote:

"Last week there was a change of all things, for the earth was opened up by heaven. Today the heavens have been cleared from the dark clouds that enshrouded them as with a heavy veil, and they proclaim the glory of God with a clear atmosphere. Today the sun rises and beams on high, rejoicing warms the earth, for there has arisen for us from the grave the real sun, Christ, and he saves all who believe on him. Today the winter of sin has stopped in repentance, and the ice of unbelief is melted by wisdom. Today spring appears spruce, and enlivens all earthly existence; the stormy winds blow gently and generate fruits, and the earth, giving nurture to the seed, brings forth the green grass. For spring is the beautiful faith in

Christ which, through baptism, produces regeneration. Today the newborn lambs and calves frisk and leap about joyfully and returning to their mothers gambol about, so that the shepherds, playing on their reeds, praise Christ in joy. Today there is a feast of regeneration for all the people who are made new by the Resurrection of Christ."

"Today"—resurrection day—"there is a feast of regeneration"—this feast—"for all who are made new by the Resurrection of Christ"—all of us.

Spring-time has come! To the wind-swept steppes of Russia, to snowy streets of America, to our cold hearts. He is risen from the dead! Take and eat!

God, help us see resurrection in every spring, help us see resurrection in every Sunday, and help us see resurrection in this feast of regeneration, through Jesus, Amen.

FIRST MEAL, LAST MEAL

So . . . she took of its fruit and ate;
and she also gave some to her husband,
who was with her, and he ate. (Genesis 3:6)

While they were eating, Jesus took bread, gave thanks
and broke it, and gave it to the disciples, saying,
"Take and eat; this is my body." (Matthew 26:26)

In the infancy paintings of the contemporary Christian artist, He Qi ("huh chee"), the baby Jesus holds a bright red apple. When the shepherds adore, he holds an apple in his little fist. When the magi bow, he holds out an apple as they hold out their gifts. On the flight to Egypt, the toddler still clings to his apple. Although He Qi's use of the apple motif is persistent and prominent, he did not invent the idea. Ever since medieval times, Christian artists have frequently placed an apple in the hand of the infant Jesus.

The apple reminds us of the first meal in Scripture, the eating of a piece of fruit in the Garden of Eden. That first meal ushered in a pattern and practice of sin that spread and intensified as humanity spread and grew. When the apple appears in Christian art in the hands of the baby Jesus, it reminds that he was born to reverse the effects of that first meal.

Years later Jesus sat at his last meal holding food

different but not disconnected from that apple. The bread and the wine, bright red as an apple, would be the symbols of the means by which Jesus would overcome the effects of that first meal—his own death.

As we sit around this table today, we see with He Qi, our fellow Christian from China, and with perceptive painters from throughout the history of Christian art, an infant holding an apple, the first fruit that led to death, and we see our Lord, the first fruits from the dead, holding the emblems of the body and blood whose breaking and shedding has rescued us from that death.

O God, forgive us not for Adam's sin but for ours, and thank you for the new Adam through whom that forgiveness flows, through Jesus, Amen.

THE FIRST MEAL ON THE MOON

And he took bread, gave thanks and broke it, and gave it to them, saying, "This is my body given for you; do this in remembrance of me." In the same way, after supper he took the cup, saying, "This cup is the new covenant in my blood, which is poured out for you." (Luke 22:19, 20)

When Neil Armstrong hop-stepped from that metal ladder to the dusty-gray surface of the moon, he said, "One small step for man, one giant step for mankind." The first man on the moon! In the midst of all the wonders of technology—booster rockets and guidance systems—it all came down to one step, one human step.

We remember that first step on the moon, but what about the first meal on the moon? The second man on the moon was Buzz Aldrin, and that first meal was . . . the Lord's Supper.

Buzz Aldrin had taken bread and wine, still common in spite of their consecration, from earth to ether, in little NASA plastic containers. Later he observed, "In the one-sixth gravity of the moon, the wine curled slowly and gracefully up the side of the cup. It is interesting to think that the first food eaten there were the elements of Holy Communion."

In the midst of all the wonders of technology—shrink-wrapped, vacuum-packed food—it all came down to bread and wine, "graceful" wine. It reminds us that that graceful cup is also a cup of grace, God's grace toward us.

Across all the expanses of time and space—across 250,000 miles and 20 centuries—the elements remain so simple, so much the same. It reminds us that God's grace is limitless, and that the table that he spreads extends even beyond this little revolving planet we ride.

It all comes down to one sip, one supper, one bite of a bit of bread, for the man on the moon, and for us. It reminds us that his grace abounds to all—all places, all times, all people.

God, help us remember that nothing, least of all time and space, can separate us from your love in Christ Jesus. And help us to always and everywhere remember that cup of your grace, through Jesus, Amen.

FIRST THANKSGIVING

They brought in the ark of God and set it inside the
tent that David had pitched for it. . . . After David had
finished sacrificing the burnt offerings and the fellowship
offerings, he blessed the people in the name of the Lord. . . .
He appointed some of the Levites to minister before
the ark of the Lord, to make petition, to give thanks,
and to praise the Lord. (1 Chronicles 16:1-4)

Over three hundred years ago a little colony of God's
people met for a thanksgiving feast. They sang and prayed
—soldiers and preachers, indigenous and immigrant,
governor and commoner. The residents brought wild turkey
and venison. The newcomers contributed geese and ducks
and fish. They baked cornbread and cooked succotash. They
gave thanks to God and shared their harvest with each
other. We call it the first thanksgiving—Plymouth,
Massachusetts, July 30, 1623. More importantly, they put
thanksgiving first.

Nearly three thousand years ago a little kingdom of
God's people met for another feast of thanksgiving. They
sang and prayed and even danced—soldiers and priests,
king and commoner. They brought lambs and bulls, bread,
raisin cakes, and date cakes. They gave thanks toward
God and shared their harvest with each other. It was a

great thanksgiving: Jerusalem, Israel, about 1000 BC. More importantly, they put thanksgiving first.

Today a little colony of God's people has gathered to give thanks—nobles and nobodies, friends and foreigners, people of every continent and country and condition. And we gather at a table, with food on it, not just a thanksgiving but a thanksgiving feast. We bring food, the fruit of the wheat and the fruit of the vine. We lift our thanks toward God and share our harvest with each other. It may not be the first thanksgiving, but it is always a great thanksgiving—(insert town, insert state, insert date). We may not be putting on the first thanksgiving, but we are trying to put thanksgiving first.

God, we pray that whenever we worship we would give thanks, and that whenever we give thanks we would gather around this table for a thanksgiving feast. Help us always to put thanksgiving first, through Jesus, Amen.

GRAIN AND GRAPES

It was now about the sixth hour, and darkness came over the whole land until the ninth hour, for the sun stopped shining. . . . Jesus called out with a loud voice, "Father, into your hands I commit my spirit." When he had said this, he breathed his last. (Luke 23:44, 46)

The great Czech artist Bohuslav Reynek loved to draw images of the farm where he lived most of his life, and he loved to make drawings of the life of Jesus. Sometimes he combined the two, picturing Mary and the baby huddled in a barn or the flight to Egypt accompanied by a farm dog or soldiers lifting Jesus to the cross from a farm wagon. Of all the scenes of Jesus' life, Reynek was most drawn to draw his crucifixion. Charcoal after charcoal shows Jesus hanging on the cross. In each of his "Crucifixions" Reynek included a darkening sun and a tawny moon hanging over the outstretched arms of the Crucified One. But in one drawing—a close-up of the disheveled head of Jesus just bowed in death—the sun and moon are replaced by a round bunch of grapes and a fanned sheaf of wheat.

What are these earthy elements doing at the crucifixion? What happened to the sun and moon, the symbols of creation sharing his suffering? They have given way to symbols of salvation, to the elements of daily life to which Jesus clung even as he let go of life. These are the images—grain and grapes—that Jesus used to foreshadow his death on the cross to the darkening minds and blood-shot eyes of his disciples. And these are the images—wheat and wine—that we still use to recall his death and recognize his presence.

When we hold the bread, we do well to peer just below to the body of Christ, to the outstretched arms of Jesus on the cross. When we cradle the cup, we do well to see in it the fruit of the vine, the blood of Christ, the source of our salvation.

O God, help us to see the cross of the crucified Christ pictured in the elements of this meal, through Jesus, Amen.

GREETING THE RISING SON

But for you who revere my name, the sun of righteousness will rise with healing in its wings. (Malachi 4:2)

In the year 1000 the people of Iceland accepted Christianity at a meeting of the clans. Decades of bloody struggle between Christian missionaries from Norway and the Icelanders who clung to the old Norse gods finally ended. The new converts to Christ soon developed a peculiar but powerful custom. When the Icelanders awoke each cold morning, and wrapped their bodies with woolens against the cold wind, and shuffled out to milk the cows or mow the hay or fish the stormy seas, they paused, turned toward the east, and faced the sun rising out of the gray northern sea into the gray northern sky. Then they crossed themselves and said, In the name of the Father and the Son and the Holy Spirit.

They looked to the east to remind themselves not of the rising sun but of the risen Son. And they crossed themselves to remember that the One who had risen had died, died on a cross, for them. They started each day remembering the death and resurrection of their Savior.

So we gather on this Lord's day, every Lord's day, to remember the resurrection of our Lord. It's our way of turning toward the east, toward the risen Son, who rose one dark dawn and rises anew across the stormy seas and lowering skies of each of our lives. And when we, the Lord's people, gather on the Lord's day, to remember the Lord's resurrection, we gather at the Lord's table to remember his death. It's our way of crossing ourselves—breaking this bread and drinking this cup—of remembering his death on that cross. It's our way of giving thanks to the Son who sacrificed himself for our sakes.

May the memory of this meal be with you each day of the week that lies ahead, as you rise to greet your life, your labors, your Lord.

God, we thank you for this bread and for this cup. May they be for us this day the eastern sky, our reminders of the death and resurrection of your Son, in whose name we pray, Amen.

HANGING ON A TREE

The God of our fathers raised Jesus from the dead—
whom you had killed by hanging him on a tree. (Acts 5:30)

The Saxons of old worshiped Woden and Thor and
Frigga and the other Germanic gods. The focus of their
worship was a Woden tree, reminding them that the god
once hung on the cosmic tree as punishment for trying
to learn the secret of death. They dispensed justice by
hanging their criminals on Woden trees.

When Charlemagne invaded Saxony and imposed his
harsh rule, he forced Christianity on the resistant Saxons.
Frankish soldiers marched them through rivers and
declared them baptized. To make the conversion clear they
also cut down the Woden trees.

In the AD 800s a missionary arrived in Saxony eager
to help the Saxons make this foreign faith their own. He
wrote down the story of Jesus—"the Best Son ever born"—
in a way they would understand. He describes how "There
on the sandy gravel they erected the gallows . . . a tree on a
mountain," and nailed him "because of jealousy and hate on
a new gallows, the wooden tree." Mockers cried out, "Here
you are: held to the gallows, broken on the tree."

There is something moving about the way that
missionary retold the story, something moving and

meaningful. It helped those skeptical Saxons, forced into the faith, see Jesus the way they had once seen their god Woden. And it helped them see Jesus the way he had once been seen—as a common criminal.

Perhaps our familiarity with the old, old story makes it hard for us to accept. Perhaps we are less moved than we should be. This is no common carpenter we remember here, but the "Best Son ever born." And yet he was a common carpenter, treated like a common criminal. Ultimately of course what we remember is that this God on a tree, this criminal on a cross, did crack the code of death, by dying for the Jews of two thousand years ago and the Saxons of a thousand years ago and all of us here and now.

Thank you, God, for raising Jesus from the dead, the one we killed by hanging him on a tree, we pray in his name, Amen.

HE BROKE IT

For I received from the Lord what I also passed on to you:
The Lord Jesus, on the night he was betrayed, took bread,
and when he had given thanks, he broke it and said,
"This is my body which is for you." (1 Corinthians 11:23, 24)

He broke it. When we break the bread, we are
participating in an act at once simple and significant. We
may not realize just how significant.

A fellow Christian from Japan writes: "Here is a strong
image of the 'broken Christ' in the ancient Christian
apostolic tradition. This broken Christ, indeed, confronts
us. But he goes further than that. By being broken he
indicates to us the new possibility of embracing others.
In my judgment here is the great spiritual message of
Christianity to humanity. One must be broken in order to
embrace others . . . . When the bread is broken, there is
created a space between the two pieces of bread. This space
is sacred. This eucharistic space is the space in which the
divine embracing of sinful humanity takes place."*

We have heard those words many times before—
"he broke it." But our Asian brother hears them a bit
differently—with the ears of a child who experienced the
firebombing of Japan, with the ears of a missionary to the
urban poor of Thailand. He sees these broken bits of bread
with eyes that have seen the brokenness of human life and

how the broken Christ embraces this broken world.

When we break bread, look not only at the emblem of the body of our broken Lord. Look also at the sacred space between one piece and the next, the space in which God embraces us all in his saving love. And look at the sacred space between one person and the next, the space we span when we pass the broken bread, from our brokenness to their brokenness. Let it be one way of embracing them in their brokenness as God has embraced us in his broken Son.

Thank you, O God, for embracing us in the brokenness of Christ. Help us become people who embrace the brokenness around us, through Jesus, Amen.

Kosuke Koyama, "The Asian Approach to Christ," Missiology *12:435-447.*

HER OWN SHARE

Instead, whoever wants to become great among you must be your servant, and whoever wants to be first must be your slave—just as the Son of Man did not come to be served, but to serve, and to give his life as a ransom for many. (Matthew 20:26-28)

We notice those who preside at the Lord's supper and those who serve the meal. But what about those who give of their time and effort to prepare the Lord's table for us every Lord's day? One Chinese woman gave of even more than her time and effort.

"We have always had floods," her husband wrote. "[I]n 1964, we had two weeks of continuous rain. When the water burst through, it could not be stopped. It wiped out everything in its path. . . . Food was scarce. In 1966, my wife passed away. She had been eating very little, letting me and the boys eat. . . . She died of starvation. We held a service to remember her. I did not officiate until . . . when the Lord's table was set. As I reached into the jar for the dry, thin biscuits, I realized there weren't enough to go round. My wife who made these biscuits had always seen to it that there was enough for everyone. . . . I still cannot figure out how she had managed to provide enough biscuits for the Lord's table when food was so scarce—unless she had added her own share."*

The story is a poignant and powerful reminder of the One who not only gave his share, but gave himself, who not only died so that we could eat, but died so that we could live. There is even a sense in which those among us who prepare this bread and cup every Sunday stand as humble reminders of the One whose body was broken and whose blood was poured out for our sakes. Remembering those among us who make sacrifices, who serve for our sakes in the name of Jesus, is one way of remembering him.

God, help us to remember that our Savior came not to be served but to serve, and help us to do the same, through Jesus, Amen.

---

*Raymond Fung, ed., Households of God on China's Soil *(Maryknoll, NY: Orbis Books, 1983).*

IN OUR GLADNESS

On the third day a wedding took place at Cana in Galilee.... This, the first of his miraculous signs, Jesus performed in Cana of Galilee. He thus revealed his glory, and his disciples put their faith in him. (John 2:1, 11)

What do we make of the miracle at the wedding feast at Cana, the miracle when those who believed the most came to believe first? We don't mind wedding feasts. We enjoy them—the processions, the swirling emotions, the good food and drink. And we don't mind Jesus being there. We're glad for Jesus to have had a good time once in a while. And we don't mind Jesus drinking wine or providing wine for others to drink. Wine was a natural part of the daily diet in Jesus' day.

But this miracle—changing water into wine to prevent embarrassment at a wedding feast—seems to pale in the presence of the "power" miracles—stilling the storm, unbinding the blind, loosing the lame, raising people from the dead. It seems a somewhat silly sign, an odd entrée into a ministry of marvelous miracles, climaxing with his own resurrection from the dead.

Why did Jesus do this seemingly insignificant miracle? The answer may come from an unlikely source, not a theologian but a novelist, Fyodor Dostoyevski, and not a commentary but a novel, *The Brothers Karamazov*. The significance of the sign, Dostoyevski says, is that God is with us in our gladness as surely as in our sadness. He is present in our times of joy as well as our times of need. God's power is present in Christ in the wedding wine just as surely as in the wailing of the wind and the wailing of the widow and the wailing of the hungry child.

God is with us in our gladness—on this glad morning, in this glad gathering of this glad community. For in this simple, glad setting, a miracle occurs, a changing, not of water to wine, but of wine to the living presence of Christ, to the living proclamation of Christ. So welcome to the feast! Welcome to the miracle! Jesus is here!

God, as we celebrate this changing, we pray that you continue to change us, through Jesus, Amen.

IN THE PRESENCE OF HIS ENEMIES

I have eagerly desired to eat this Passover with you before I suffer. . . . But the hand of him who is going to betray me is with mine on the table. (Luke 22:15, 21)

Polycarp, the bishop of Smyrna, was a disciple of the apostle John. He was a link between Christ's apostles and the second-century Christians trying to maintain faith in an age of heresy and hardship. When orders came for the arrest of the eighty-seven year-old leader in AD 165, friends begged Polycarp to flee. He moved from farmhouse to farmhouse, until he was eventually arrested, taken back to Smyrna, tied to a stake, and stabbed to death by the executioner.

But it is not the life of Polycarp or his death that interests us as we gather at this table. It is what he did just before his arrest. When soldiers approached the farmhouse where he was hiding, Polycarp welcomed them, seated them around the table, and served them a meal. It was his last supper, but he spent it serving others, his enemies. As he began his trek through the valley of the shadow of death, he prepared a table for others in the presence of his enemies.

Just before his arrest Jesus also hosted a meal. He invited others, those who would deny him, those who would betray him. And he served them, washing their feet, sharing his food. It was his last supper, but he spent it serving others, his betrayers.

In the story of Polycarp we see ourselves as those enemies of Christ whom he came to serve. But in the story of Polycarp we also see ourselves as those whom Jesus has called to serve others. The person who passes you the food might just act like they never knew you someday, might betray your trust someday, might turn on you someday. We sit at this table as those who were once the enemies of our host and we sit here in the presence of our enemies, like Polycarp, like Jesus, sharing, serving.

God, help us welcome others with mercy, help us to serve others with humility, and help us to share this meal in love, in his name, Amen.

JUDAS' EYES, JESUS' EYES

And he took bread, gave thanks and broke it,
and gave it to them, saying, "This is my body given for
you; do this in remembrance of me." In the same way,
after the supper he took the cup, saying, "This cup is the
new covenant in my blood, which is poured out for you.
But the hand of him who is going to betray me
is with mine on the table." (Luke 22:19-21)

In the oldest church in Singapore, built in 1835, hangs a large painting of the Last Supper. It seems fairly typical. Jesus sits at the table with his disciples. His left hand holds a loaf. His right hand is poised near a cup. His eyes are aimed slightly upward, pensive, prayerful. The disciples are variously angled and grouped. Some look at Jesus, some at each other, all startled, evidently at the unspeakable news that one of them would betray him.

But one feature sets this painting apart from others. This painting from halfway around the world shows Judas, sitting across from Jesus, turned halfway around on the bench, staring straight into the eyes of the viewer. Try as we might to look elsewhere, our eyes are drawn back to those riveting, regretful eyes. They stare deep into ours, awakening the possibility of our own betrayal.

What's amazing is that the betrayer was at the table at all. And if Judas' eyes are any indication, so are we. We stand just a few feet away, in the same shadowed room, not driven from the table but drawn to it by other eyes that forgive rather than accuse.

Today we see the eyes of Jesus—staring back at us in the fragments of bread, reflected in the fruit of the vine. They remind us to repent. Those mercifully sad eyes also call us to remember other words of Jesus—not only "One of you will betray me," but "This is my body broken for you" and "This cup that is poured out for you is the new covenant in my blood."

God, if this meal causes us to regret, let it also call us to remember, not only our sin, but also our salvation, through Jesus, Amen.

THE KING OF THE HAWAIIANS

The Word became flesh and made his dwelling among us.
(John 1:14)

And they sang a new song: "You are worthy to take the scroll and to open its seals, because you were slain, and with your blood you purchased men for God from every tribe and language and people and nation." (Revelation 5:9)

Depictions of their ancient kings are all over the Hawaiian Islands, with their almond eyes and koa-dark skin and cheekbones precipitous as a crater. They all wore the royal robe—a cape woven of tiny red and yellow feathers plucked by islanders, a few from each tropical bird they would trap and release.

So it's not hard to recognize the Hawaiian king in the stained glass window in the Palapala Hoomau Congregational Church on the eastern end of Maui. He has the eyes, the cheeks, the skin; the long black hair and the short black beard; and of course the red and yellow cape.

But it is not King Ka-meha-meha—the First, the Second, the Third, or the Fourth! It is King Jesus, with downcast eyes and a down-reaching hand. The window is enlightening, the way it sheds light on how God's glory was filtered through flesh, on how God became one of us, one with us, us Jews, us Hawaiians, us Japanese, us Americans.

This meal is also a window on how God not only came among us but became one with us, in life and death and life again. Here we celebrate the fantastic fact that when he sits at this table with us he looks like us, all of us, each of us.

Here at this table is where we remind ourselves that God became like us, a flesh-and-blood, infant-adolescent-adult, live-till-he-died human being. And we remind ourselves that God came among us, all of the whoever-we-are, however-different-from-one-another-we-are human beings.

This is his body, broken for all of us. This cup is the new covenant in his blood, reconciling us to God and us to us.

God, we thank you for the good news that the Word not only became flesh but dwelled and dwells among us, all of us, through Jesus, Amen.

MARCHING WITH THE CROSS

Then he called the crowd to him along with his disciples and said: "If anyone would come after me, he must deny himself and take up his cross and follow me." (Mark 8:34)

She lived through decades of persecution, forced into menial labor in mines or fields, under constant surveillance, constant threat, constant fear. She was from North Korea and she was a Christian. Thousands of Christians survived the purge of 1958, holding fast to their faith, living out their faith, spreading their faith. Possession of a Bible or a cross was grounds for severe punishment.

She sometimes wondered how she and her fellow Christians survived. She recalled years of hidden tears, of silent—always silent—prayers. She knew the Bible well and never missed Sunday worship. She tied her simple belongings in a cloth bearing the words, "Believe in the Lord Jesus, and you will be saved—you and your household"—longing for the day when she could cry out "Hallelujah" or say the name of Jesus in public. Most of all, she said, she would have liked to march down the street with the cross.

Part of what we do at this table is recognize Jesus, who lived his life under surveillance and threat, who marched down a street with a cross and suffered its severe punishment. But part of what we do here is recognize the other saints who gather Sunday by Sunday in sundry places around the world, places where it is not always easy to eat.

We remember not only the broken body of Jesus, but also our fellow believers who partake in pain. We remember not only the one who shed his blood for us, but also all the ones who face bloodshed with unfaltering faith.

The next time we say "Jesus" or "Hallelujah," we might think not only of our Savior, but also of his silent saints in North Korea. And we might let the memory of one faithful lady, as well as the memory of our Lord, teach us what it means to "march down the street with the cross."

God, give us the resolve to live for you boldly, to carry the cross courageously, and to follow you faithfully, through Jesus, Amen.

MICHELANGELO'S MASTERPIECE

I eagerly expect and hope that I will in no way be ashamed, but will have sufficient courage so that now as always Christ will be exalted in my body, whether by life or by death. For to me, to live is Christ and to die is gain.
(Philippians 1:20, 21)

It isn't the ceiling of the Sistine Chapel, or "The Last Judgment" on the wall at the end of that great hall, but it's still a masterpiece. It's a simple, little masterpiece by Michelangelo.

It's only a sketch, a red-pencil sketch—one scene, a resurrection, sketched over another scene, a burial. They were drawn together, by the same artist, with the same pencil, on the same piece of paper—the death-demanded burial, and the red-dawn-drawn resurrection. But although the burial scene is plainly the burial of Jesus, the resurrection is not his. It is the resurrection of his dear friend, Lazarus.

Why did the master piece the death and burial of the one who would rise to be exalted together with the resurrection of one who would rise only to die again? We do not know. But we do know that the death of Jesus was not just for himself, for the one who died to live. It was for those of us who live to die.

This meal is not only the remembrance of Jesus' death and burial acted out in anticipation of the happy ending of his resurrection. It is the remembrance of his death and burial re-enacted in the realization that we who have been called into new life in Christ will yet die in Christ.

It reminds us that we who will die in Christ will yet live in him. It reminds us to join with Paul in saying, "For to me, to live is Christ and to die is gain." This meal, like Michelangelo's double drawing, his little masterpiece, reminds us that our life and death and life overlap his because his, thankfully, overlapped ours.

God, we who are about to die salute you, and we who are about to live celebrate you. Help us see our whole existence in the experience of your Son who died and now lives, through Jesus, Amen.

A MONSOON MEAL

He saw the disciples straining at the oars, because the wind was against them. About the fourth watch of the night he went out to them, walking on the lake.... They cried out, because they all saw him and were terrified. Immediately he spoke to them and said, "Take courage! It is I. Don't be afraid." Then he climbed into the boat with them, and the wind died down. (Mark 6:48-51)

The monsoon rains drowned out all sound—the songs of the bird, the flip-flop of the sandals of the people of the Indian village splish-splashing their way to the church building. It was small and plain, gray blocks under a gray tin roof in the gray rain. The gray even seemed to permeate the lightless church. But when the worshipers slipped inside and slipped off their plastic ponchos, a riot of colorful clothes emerged and a cacophony of cheerful chatter began. It almost drowned out the rain that drummed on the roof. Then the voices of the worshipers—workers on the tea plantation whose little leaves danced in the driving rain— joined joyously in praise of God. The jumble of mumbled prayers and the powerful preaching competed with the rat-a-tat rain. But when Communion came, the villagers fell silent on their woven mats, while the flat Indian bread and watered-down wine were passed, and the monsoon mounted to their ears again. The storm never sounded louder than in the silence of the Lord's supper.

That's the way it was for the disciples in the boat. They encountered the presence of Jesus not after the stilling of the storm but in the midst of it. While the storm still raged around them, Jesus, who had stilled a storm for them once, now stalked the storm with them.

And that's the way it is for us at this table, this commemoration of Jesus' death. We hear the persistent pounding of our own perversity, our sin, louder than ever, but we also hear the windy word of God's grace—Jesus has saved us from our sins.

God, help us to live from the It-is-I presence of this table into the stormy weather that lies ahead, through Jesus, Amen.

A MONUMENT TO LOVE

**Greater love has no one than this,
that he lay down his life for his friends.** (John 15:13)

When he inherited the throne of northern India
from his Mongol predecessors in 1630, the new emperor
gave himself the name Shah Jahan, King of the World.
History remembers him less for his conquests than for
his constructions, especially the Taj Mahal. Shah Jahan's
beloved wife, Mumatz Mahal, died bearing his fourteenth
child. To preserve her memory he built as her tomb
what may be the most famous building in the world. It
is certainly the most beautiful. It rises like a milky pearl
from the red dust of the north Indian desert, lustrous white
marble, perfectly proportioned, stunningly situated. Its
only decoration, other than the sensuous shape of its dome
and its sunset glow, is the dark, detailed inlay of quotations
from the Koran.

When one of the Emperor's sons emerged victorious
from a civil war for control of the throne, he placed his
father under house arrest for the last eight years of his
life in a tower apartment of his own fortress. The only
accommodation to the wishes of the former Shah was a
window that allowed him to gaze down the river on the Taj
Mahal, his great monument to his greatest love.

This table is no mausoleum. Jesus' tomb is empty

and he is present with us in this present moment. It is no mausoleum, but it is a monument, a memorial. At this table we remember the person and passion of Jesus. It is no work of architectural art. Except for its exceptional purpose, there is nothing exceptional about it. And yet people come to see it and to sense its significance again and again. Whatever else it is or is not, this table is about love—our love for someone who loved us so much that he gave his life to give us birth. Where we live matters little, as long as we are in seeing distance, in eating distance, of this table. This table, simple as it is, is our monument to love.

God, thank you for Jesus, a person, not a place, but still the monument to your love, in his name, Amen.

NAKED AT THE CROSS

The Spirit of the Lord is on me, because he has anointed
me to preach good news to the poor. He has sent me
to proclaim freedom for the prisoners and recovery
of sight for the blind, to release the oppressed. (Luke 4:18)

The painting of Jesus on the cross by contemporary
Chinese Christian artist He Qi ("huh chee") challenges us
to think more deeply about the meaning of the crucifixion.
In his own vibrant style he combines traditional features of
western Christian art with distinctively Chinese features.
But nothing can really prepare us for this painting.

Jesus' mother stands at the foot of the cross. Her head
is pitched back, her mouth agape, as her agony over the
agony of her son escapes in a scream. She holds a baby,
the corpse of a baby. In her eyes he was still that baby that
she had nurtured and prepared for a career that led to this
cross. No wonder she cries.

Others crowd around the cross, but not the
conventional characters of Western art—no John the
Baptist, no John the apostle, no Roman soldiers or Jewish
religious leaders. Here stands a blind man in need of sight.
Here lies a man disabled or dead, in need of healing or life.
Here stands a man behind bars in need of liberation. The
artist reminds us of all those Jesus came for, lived for, and
died for.

But the most striking feature of He Qi's "Crucifixion" is Mary Magdalene who stands naked at the foot of the cross.

At first glance we are scandalized. But those of us who gather at this table, who come to the cross often enough, know exactly what he means. To gather at this table, to stand at the cross, means to strip away all the pretensions, all our shameful past, all our prideful present. Mary was a sinner who had allowed Jesus to strip herself of herself. So are we. So must we—stand naked at the foot of the cross and be clothed in his righteousness alone.

Accept us now, O God, naked as we are. As we eat and drink, may we put on Christ, in his name we pray, Amen.

NOT JUST WORDS

"Take and eat; this is my body." "Drink from it, all of you. This is my blood of the covenant, which is poured out for many for the forgiveness of sins." (Matthew 26:26-28)

"Jesus hiked on up from the Samaritans at Sichar to his home pad area around the Sea of Galilee. And he walked into a fair dinkum home-town welcome. The news of the punch-up at the temple in Jerusalem had spread like a bush fire and the crowd in the cheap seats went for it with their ears back." That's the way an Australian fisherman rewords the gospel in a book called *The Day the Grog Ran Out.**

Most of the wording of the story of the Last Supper has also been altered to Aussie fisherman dialect. "In the middle of the buzz, Judas asked Jesus, 'Master, is it I?' Jesus said. . . , 'Your own lips have said it.' Then he told Judas to scram and get it over with. Judas left. . . . As Judas was the bloke that looked after their dough, they thought Jesus must have sent him off to drum up a bit more tucker or something."

But there in the midst of all those down-under, down-home colloquialisms, it says: "Jesus took bread, and blessed and broke it, and gave it to his disciples, saying, Take, eat, this is my body, given for you; do this for the commemoration of me.' Then he took a cup of wine. 'Drink, all of you, of this; for this is my blood, of the new testament, shed for many for the remission of sins. Do this, whenever you drink it, for a commemoration of me.'"

It makes you think those words are not "just words." They are not negotiable even in the slang of an Australian fisherman. Whatever else we say at the table of our Lord we should always and at least say these words—This is his body, given for you. This cup is the New Testament in his blood.

God, we thank you for the Word, and for the words that are not just words, through Jesus, Amen.

Keith Murray, The Day the Grog Ran Out and Other Stories from the Big Book *(New York: HarperCollins, 1986).*

A PART OF THE WHOLE

So in Christ we who are many form one body, and each member belongs to all the others. (Romans 12:5)

The young Indian tour guide at the beautiful Taj Mahal was married and had a young son. The boy's name? "Ansh." Was that a family name or a common name in northern India? No, the young man admitted, he had never heard the word used as a name. What did it mean? "A part, a part of the whole." Why such a name? Because, the young man replied, I want my son to remember that, wherever he goes and whatever he does, he is always a part of our family.

One of the things we do when we gather at this table is remind ourselves that we are part of one family, one body. We are individuals, each with our own identities and personalities and occupations, each with our own names. But when we eat and drink together we remember that, wherever we are and whatever else we are doing, we are a part of the family of God, a part of the body of Christ. We are all "Ansh."

The salvation we celebrate means not only rescue from a life of sin but also incorporation into the Savior—we are in Christ. But our common salvation also means that we who have become a part of Christ have also become a part of all those who have become a part of Christ. "We, who are many, are one body in Christ, and individually we are members of one another."

The reality of our "membership" in Christ and with one another gives us a new and more meaningful way to think about the many Christians around the world who are communing at the Lord's table today. But it should also give us a new way of thinking about the people sitting next to us and around us. Each of us could at least for a few moments forget the names that distinguish us from one another and call each other "Ansh," a part, a part of the whole.

God, help us commune with one another even as we commune with Christ, Amen.

A PLACE OF PEACE

I have told you these things, so that in me you may
have peace. In this world you will have trouble.
But take heart! I have overcome the world! (John 16:33)

Magnus was the son of a Norwegian earl who ruled the
northern islands of Scotland nearly nine hundred years
ago. In a world of war, young Magnus found a place of
peace in the monastery school. On those rock-cold coasts he
fostered a peaceful heart.

The king of Norway forced the earl's son to join his
raids along the coast of England. One day the king ordered
all hands to arm themselves and prepare for battle with
two Welsh warships. While the battle raged around him,
Magnus took a book of the Psalms, sat down on the deck,
and began to sing. When the king challenged him, he
responded, "I have no quarrel with these men and I will
not fight them." The king promised to deal later with this
boy who refused to fight. That night Magnus slipped off the
ship and swam to the English shore. Years later Magnus
finally returned to rule his island homeland. But that day,
on a pitching deck, in the midst of a pitched battle, he
found a place of peace.

This table is a place of peace. The world is still a place
of war and conflict, of aggression and oppression. People
still make unreasonable demands on us that go against

God's will. But this table is a place of peace in the midst of a climate of conflict.

Peace is precisely what Jesus prayed for in the upper room. On the night on which he broke bread and poured the cup, he prayed for peace. The peace he prayed for is a peace that does not necessarily still the storms of war but gives us respite in the midst of storms. So we gather, remembering young Magnus, sitting on the deck of a warship, in the midst of battle, singing the Psalms. And we gather in this place of peace, remembering our Prince of Peace, resolving to practice peace.

God of peace, we pray for peace, from wars that rage within and without, through Jesus, Amen.

THE SADDEST PLACE IN THE WORLD

His purpose was to create in himself one new man out of the two, thus making peace, and in this one body to reconcile both of them to God through the cross, by which he put to death their hostility. (Ephesians 2:15, 16)

On the coast of Ghana stands a fortress built to guard the gold Europeans extracted from "gold coast" mines. A few decades later the fortress's airless chambers began to store a different commodity—slaves. In the same spaces where gold was once heaped, human bodies now lay crowded and cramped, some sick, some dying, some painfully alive. In the midst of this rectangle of rooms, dark and dank, was a large whitewashed courtyard open to the warm breezes of the beautiful Ghanaian coast. And in the middle of that courtyard stood a church where Christians— set free by Christ but now capturing and trading in human flesh—gathered for worship. They praised the Creator and communed with Jesus, while all around them human suffering of their own making went on unabated. It is one of the saddest places in the world.

We sit here today worshiping and commemorating, while all around us human suffering, possibly even suffering of our own making, goes on. To gather here oblivious to the suffering of our Savior would be a terrible travesty, but to gather here oblivious to the suffering of others would be a tragedy of like proportion. Their suffering may be financial or physical, social or psychological or spiritual. They may be enslaved by forces of their own making or of circumstances over which none of us has control. God forbid that their suffering be a result of our complicity!

So we gather today resolved to remember Jesus who suffered not only because of us but for us. And we gather resolved to remember that we who were once enslaved in the fortresses of sin and self and death now stand in the exhilarating freedom of salvation in Christ. And we gather at this table today resolved to remember that we who have been liberated must never be party to the enslavement of those around us.

God, thank you for setting the captives—including us—free, through Jesus, Amen.

THE SHEPHERD WEARS A CROWN

I am the good shepherd. The good shepherd lays down his life for the sheep. (John 10:11)

On the back wall of the old church, behind the baptistery, is a three-paneled stained-glass window of Jesus the Good Shepherd. On the left the shepherd is clinging to a cliff, holding onto the gnarled roots that hold a lost lamb. He reaches out precariously but determinedly. The lamb's life is at risk. But so is his. This picture of the reaching, rescuing shepherd is surrounded by a vine, a grapevine. The Lord's Supper reminds us of risk, of rescue, of redemption.

In the right panel the shepherd is leading the flock back into the fold. But there is something strange about the shepherd. The shepherd wears a crown. The king of Israel was often portrayed as a shepherd of God's people. But this crown is a crown of thorns. This shepherd is the one who lays down his life for the sheep. And this panel is also surrounded by a grapevine. The Lord's Supper reminds us of his crown, of his suffering, of his death.

In the center stands the good shepherd in the midst of his flock. He cradles a lamb, perhaps the rescued lamb. But there is something odd about his eyes. They do not look up to the God who sent him nor down at the sheep looking up at their shepherd. Instead they appear to look down at the baptistery, always on the lookout for the lost who have found their way to the watering hole, to the place of deliverance. And there in the window with the downward-cast but not downcast eyes are the symbols of the supper—sheaves of wheat and a cup—reminding us that when we flock around this table we remember a shepherd who cares about our lost-ness.

We meet at this table with none other than the shepherd himself, the bread of life, remembering that it is for us that the shepherd wears a crown.

God, we thank you for the Shepherd of our souls, in whose name we gather, for his bread-like body, his crushed-grape blood, his death, his life, in his name, Amen.

SLAVE TO THE SLAVES

For even the Son of Man did not come to be served, but to serve, and to give his life as a ransom for many. (Mark 10:45)

In 1610 the Spaniard Peter Claver became a missionary to the people of Cartagena, Colombia. What Claver found in that bustling seaport was a center of the New World slave trade. Only about a third of the "cargo" survived the horrors of trans-Atlantic transport. The rest were emaciated, riddled with disease. They feared death, but a worse fate awaited. They were sold as slaves to toil in the fields or work in the mines, kept alive only to labor, considered creatures, hardly human, by their owners.

Claver, who had dedicated himself as a slave to God, now declared himself "*aethiopum semper servus,*" Latin for "always a slave to the Africans." For the next forty-four years he was a slave to the slaves. He met every slave ship, paddling out in a canoe, first with food, then with medicine. Day by day he visited the holding cells where the slaves awaited auction, teaching them about Jesus through a team of trained African interpreters, baptizing converts, continuing to minister to the sick. He persisted in offering slaves Communion in spite of fellow Christians who attacked him for profaning the Lord's table by offering Sacraments to creatures with barely a soul. On Christian holy days Claver prepared great banquets to which he invited Cartagena's slaves and beggars, even its lepers.

We would do well to mimic this Jesuit who mimicked Jesus. We too have been called to minister to the neediest among us, the rejected, the repressed. We might meet them first with food, any food, to allay the deep hunger of starving people all around the world, even around us. We might meet them with the gospel, feeding their souls with the love and acceptance we have experienced in Christ. We might open our banquets to beggars, our potlucks to the poor. And we might remember that this table is open to all.

Now God, help us remember that we gather at this meal, once slaves to sin, now slaves to God, emancipated by our Servant-Savior Jesus to be slaves of one another, Amen.

SOMETHING'S FISHY

Jesus then took the loaves, gave thanks, and distributed to those who were seated as much as they wanted. He did the same with the fish. (John 6:11)

And he took bread, gave thanks and broke it, and gave it to them, saying, "This is my body which is given for you." (Luke 22:19)

Jesus came, took the bread and gave it to them, and did the same with the fish. (John 21:13)

Something's fishy about that painting of the Last Supper. It's not just how old it is—thirteenth century—or how small. It's not just Jesus' face—serious and serene but not severe. Nor his hands—one stroking the head of John the beloved, the other handing a morsel to the mouth of Judas the betrayer. It's not the round table, tilted toward the viewer, or the shocked expressions on the disciples' faces. But something's still fishy.

It's the menu! Among the bowls of new-covenant wine and my-body bread are two bowls full of fish. Something's fishy at the Last Supper.

But the fish reminds us of an earlier meal, a meal of compassion, when thousands of hungry stomachs and souls were fed on a menu of bread and fish and became convinced that this Feeder was none other than their Leader, this Server was their Savior.

And the fish "preminds" us of a yet later meal, a meal of companionship, when a few hungry stomachs and spirits were filled with a menu of bread and fish and became convinced that the one who crouched on the shore of the sea was the one they had seen crucified, that this short-order cook had become, in short order, the risen Lord.

Something's wonderfully fishy in this old depiction of the Last Supper. It reminds us that the One we remember has compassion on our hungers, that the One we gather with was crucified in our behalf, and that the one who calls us to the breakfast table is none other than the really risen Lord.

God, help us as we eat the bread and drink the cup to focus on the one who feeds us, body, soul, and spirit, through Jesus, Amen.

SPEAKING HIS LANGUAGE

He came and preached peace to you who were
far away and peace to those who were near.
For through him we both have access to the Father by
one Spirit. Consequently, you are no longer foreigners
and aliens, but fellow citizens with God's people
and members of God's household. (Ephesians 2:17-19)

The traveler from the United States had managed to
find what he had been looking for, something not on the
tourist maps—a church where he could worship and most
importantly share the Lord's Supper with fellow Christians
in this bustling, far-from-home city of Athens. He found
it on a list of churches posted in the hotel—*Ekklesia
Christou*, "Church of Christ." He wrote down the address
as accurately as he could and handed it to a taxi driver
who found it finally—with a good deal of horn-honking—on
Hermes Street. He walked up to the apartment converted
into a church building on the second story over the Sunday-
silent shop.

The welcome was warm, the prayers were earnest, the
special music was heart-felt, and the sermon was obviously
thoughtful and powerful. But the visitor to this gathering
of Christians half-way across this walking-in-its-sleep city,
half-way around the world from his not-yet-waking-from-
its-sleep home congregation, understood nothing. Even

the words at the Lord's table were a mystery—no, not a mystery, which they always are in any language, they were simply incomprehensible.

The mystery was that when the grizzled old man with the gnarled hands and gap-toothed grin tore the bread and poured the cup and passed among the congregants with the emblems of the Lord's body, the visitor suddenly comprehended, comprehended what they were doing, comprehended what they were thinking. And in comprehending their thoughts and actions he comprehended the Christ whose death they remembered and reenacted and celebrated. The Lord's Supper is self-explanatory to a believer. This meal needs no interpreter, no United Nations headphones. This table is its own translation.

When the visitor handed the emblems back to the gap-toothed old man, he too smiled, smiled because at last he was speaking his language.

God, thank you for speaking our language in Jesus, and for allowing us to speak each other's language in this meal, through Jesus, Amen.

STANDING UP TOGETHER

But we had to celebrate and be glad, because
this brother of yours was dead and is alive again;
he was lost and is found. (Luke 15:32)

Along River Street in Savannah, where African slaves were once offloaded and marketed to American plantation owners, stands a touching statue of an African-American slave family, bent, huddled, but well-dressed, standing firm, standing together. Below the sculpture these words by Maya Angelou are inscribed. "We were stolen, sold, and bought together from the African continent. We got on the slave ships together. We lay back to belly in the holds of the slave ships. . . . Sometimes [we] died together, and our lifeless bodies thrown overboard together. Together we are standing up together, with faith and even joy." Of all the evocative words in this inscription—stolen, sold, bought, lifeless—the author chose to highlight the often repeated "together." Every part of the slave experience—ripped from their homes and homelands, hauled hundreds of miserable miles across the sea in discomfort and disease, dying in droves, only to be sold into crushing conditions—they suffered together. But their descendants also share a common experience: they share the memory, they preserve a faith, and they even rekindle a kind of joy—together.

Today around every Communion table in every church

there stands a touching monument. The monument is not so much the table itself or even, only, the objects on the table. It is the people around the table—well-dressed people, bent by the pressures of the past, huddled in their hardships, standing or sitting together. They had once been sold to sin, enslaved in sin. Many have found themselves in a far country of the soul, spiritually dead. But now they are gathered around a common table, eating and drinking a common meal—together. We are that people. And when we gather here we share a common experience. We share the memory of a Master who suffered for the sake of his servants. We preserve a faith in our Captain. And, in spite of the persecutions of the past or the fears of the future, we rekindle joy—together.

Keep us in Christ, O God, and keep us together, in memory, in faith, and in joy, through Jesus, Amen.

STRAPPED TO THE CROSS

I urge you, brothers, in view of God's mercy, to offer your
bodies as living sacrifices, holy and pleasing to God—
this is your spiritual act of worship. (Romans 12:1)

His paintings grace the walls of the world's finest
museums. But only one depicts a Biblical scene. His
realistic landscapes inspired a whole generation of
twentieth-century artists. But only one was a Biblical
landscape. The great American artist Thomas Eakins
was both influential and popular. But he painted only one
painting with a religious theme. It was a crucifixion.

In order to paint the death of Jesus in all its human
realism, Eakins built a life-sized cross. Then he strapped
a young art student to its beams by his hands and feet.
Finally he painted what he saw—the pained face, the
hung head, the twisted torso, the bent knees, the contorted
fingers. The result is a strikingly realistic portrayal of the
death-agony of Jesus.

This painting hangs in our minds as a reminder
of what we do at this table. Here we repaint our own
rendition of the crucifixion. Our brush is a broken loaf of
bread. Our pigment is grape-red. Our canvas is the all-too-
real landscape of our lives. Our model is Jesus, really dead.

And if we should ever find ourselves forgetting that the

crucifixion was a deed, not just a doctrine, that the really-human carpenter really hung on a cross, we would do well to follow the method of Thomas Eakins. We have only to, as it were, rebuild the beams of this table into the beams of a cross and strap ourselves to it and see in the sacrifice of our lives a very visual proclamation of the sacrifice of Jesus, the pain-love of God.

And so we take this bread-brush from his contorted fingers, and we take the cup containing his blood-red palette from his holey hands, from one crucified life to another, and we remember that this meal is really all about sacrifice—his and ours.

God, accept our imperfectly painted lives as a sacrifice to you, not on the basis of what we have done but what you have done, through Jesus, in whose name we pray, Amen.

THEY STILL ATE

For whenever you eat this bread and drink this cup,
you proclaim the Lord's death until he comes.
(1 Corinthians 11:26)

Christianity flourished in Japan from 1570 until 1614, when it was cruelly and decisively repressed. For the next two centuries missionaries were denied entrance and Christians were not allowed to practice their faith. Those who persisted were publicly executed. Some were wrapped in mats and thrown into the sea, some were buried to their necks on the seashore to await the incoming tide, and some were crucified. The Lord's Supper was strictly forbidden. As far as anyone knew, Christianity was totally stamped out in Japan.

But when in the late 1800s Japan was reopened to the wider world, an amazing discovery was made. Thousands, tens of thousands of *Kakure Kirishitan*, hidden Christians, emerged, professing a faith that had been passed down for generations. They still worshipped God and believed in Jesus. They still knelt before the cross, hidden in a niche behind their Buddhist shrine. And they still celebrated the Lord's Supper. Every Christmas Eve they gathered secretly in small groups to remember Jesus' death on the eve of his birth. On the low table before them these hidden Christians placed three bowls of rice and three cups of sake (pronounced **sah**-kee), Japanese rice wine. Then they ate. No matter how repressed they were, no matter how much they forgot, they still ate.

The hidden Christians of Japan remind us that no matter how easily or often we take the Lord's Supper, we must still remember its meaning and its purpose. We do more here than reminisce. We do more here than repeat. We re-encounter the Christ who was born in our midst and died for our sakes. And we proclaim that death, proclaim it by our very practice.

So whether with bread or rice, with grape juice or sake, in the open or in secret, this meal gives us a way of seeing through the surface, of looking through the layers of cultural expectations to the core, to the cross, to the Christ.

Thank you, O God, for the persistence of faith, faith focused on these evidences of your love in Christ, we pray through him, Amen.

THUNDER AT THE RIVER

We were therefore buried with him through baptism
into death in order that, just as Christ was raised
from the dead through the glory of the Father,
we too may live a new life. (Romans 6:4)

For whenever you eat this bread and drink this cup,
you proclaim the Lord's death until he comes.
(1 Corinthians 11:26)

They traveled deep into China to meet with two house
churches—teaching the Christians, evangelizing the
seekers. It rained the whole day-long drive. But once there
the sky cleared and the worship lasted into the night. Early
the next morning they went to the swollen Pearl River for
eight baptisms. Thunder, lightning, and a fierce rainstorm
arrived with them. Thunder—like the thunderous voice
that resounded, This is my beloved Son, in whom I am well
pleased. Lightning—like the bright Spirit-dove alighting
lightly on Jesus. The rain left them all soaked, sharing as it
were in their own bedraggled way the baptisms of the new
believers. Then the sun came out and they all celebrated
these eight births with a feast at a local teahouse.

What more appropriate thing to do after a baptism
than to have a feast? It may be at a Chinese teahouse or at
a carry-out picnic or at a carry-in dinner in the fellowship
hall. But new life is worth celebrating by the whole church,

maybe even several congregations together.

On the other hand what more appropriate thing to do at the Lord's Supper than to remember your baptism? It may not have involved thunder and lightning, only the quiet assurance that God works wonders in lives yielded fully to him. It may not have been a raging river, only the reminder that baptism is always a death-defying act and that our baptisms are less a response to Jesus' baptism than to his death. The important thing is to remember that we were baptized into his death and that here at this feast it is his death that we proclaim. At the river, at the feast— the two just go together. The two must go together.

God, as we gather at this table, help us remember our baptisms, and our Savior, and his death, through Jesus, Amen.

TOKENS OF TRIUMPH

Therefore, when Christ came into the world he said:
". . . I have come to do your will, O God." "And by that will,
we have been made holy through the sacrifice of the
body of Jesus Christ once for all." (Hebrews 10:5,7,10)

One of the oldest Christian documents in English is a powerful poem called "The Dream of the Rood." Rood means cross. Written in England in the AD 600s, it contains three wonderful insights into the cross of Christ.

First, the cross itself, now often covered with gold and jewels, was once rough-hewn and bloody. The poet describes the cross as if it shared the sufferings of Christ: "Long years ago . . . /They hewed me down on the edge of the holt,/Severed my trunk; strong foemen took me,/. . . a gallows for rogues./High on their shoulders they bore me to hilltop,/Fastened me firmly, an army of foes." By thinking of the cutting down of the cross, we think of Jesus, we picture his pain.

Second, although the death was God's will, it had to be Jesus' choice: "Then I saw the King of all mankind/ In brave mood hasting to mount upon me." "Then the young Warrior, God, the All-Wielder,/Put off His raiment, steadfast and strong;/With lordly mood in the sight of many/He mounted the Cross to redeem mankind." Jesus

chose the cross, going to his sacrificial death voluntarily—
"Not my will but thine be done."

Third, like the tree in the poem, we share Christ's
scorn; we feel his pain. We have been cut down and made to
bear the taunts of tormenters. Like the cross, we who were
rough and bloody have been rendered glorious by the blood
of Christ. Like Christ, we chose to be chosen, we willed to
be washed in the blood of the Lamb.

"The Dream of the Rood" calls the cross "that token
of triumph." But so are these—this bread and this cup—
tokens of the triumph that began with his saving death
and ended with his victorious resurrection. So celebrate the
cross, celebrate Christ, and celebrate these tokens of his
triumph.

*God, may we, like the cross, bear in our bodies the
marks of Christ, the wounds by which we are healed,
through Jesus, Amen.*

TRAVELING BY STARLIGHT

For God so loved the world that he gave his one and only Son, that whoever believes in him shall not perish but have eternal life. For God did not send his Son into the world to condemn the world, but to save the world through him. (John 3:16, 17)

About AD 110 in the ancient city of Antioch, a revered Christian leader named Ignatius wrote these words:

"A star shone forth in the heaven above all the stars; and its light was unutterable, and its strangeness caused amazement; and all the rest of the constellations with the sun and moon formed themselves into a chorus about the star; but the star itself far outshone them all; and there was perplexity to know whence came this strange appearance which was so unlike them . . . , when God appeared in the likeness of man unto the newness of everlasting life. . . . " (*To the Ephesians,* 19)

Ignatius wrote words about a birth on his way to his death, traveling under Roman guard to his martyrdom in Rome. Ignatius wrote words about the Bethlehem sky full of stars on his way to a stadium full of beasts. And he recognized that the star of stars not only signaled incarnation—God appearing in human likeness—it also signaled eternity—"the newness of everlasting life."

We too are on a journey, a journey with Jesus. We too are on a journey toward death, toward life. And as we travel, we would do well to remember the focus of our fellow traveler—on Jesus, on the brightness of his star, on his humanity, on his suffering, on his glory.

So we gather today to remember Jesus—his journey and ours, his suffering and ours, his glory and ours. We gather to commemorate birth and death, the coming of the incarnate Christ and the presence of the crucified Christ, all in this one act of worship.

This is his once-born body, broken for us. This is the cup of the Christmas-to-crucifixion covenant in his blood. We pause to partake, celebrating his birth, remembering his death, and anticipating life, everlasting life.

God, we take these tokens of his death as a token of his birth and of ours as well, through Jesus, Amen.

UNBINDING THEIR FEET

It is for freedom that Christ has set us free. . . .
But do not use your freedom to indulge the sinful nature
rather, serve one another in love. (Galatians 5:1,13)

When Christian missionaries reentered China in
the nineteenth century, they confronted unique forms of
repression. Women were forbidden any role in government
service. Formal education for women simply did not exist.
Social contacts outside the family circle were discouraged.
Husbands were free to take concubines. The killing of
female babies was legal and routine. Last but not least was
a practice that may seem less offensive but actually stood
as the symbol of the institutionalized inferiority of women
in China—foot-binding.

The gospel had a positive and positively liberating
effect in many of these areas. But the most direct impact
was on foot-binding. In 1874 Christian missionaries and
their converts founded a society for its suppression. In 1902
the practice was abolished.

But more important than any government edict was
a wonderful practice that developed in the churches. As
women approached the baptistery to confess their faith in
Christ and be incorporated into him, they paused, stooped
down, and unbound their bent and shriveled feet, for the

first time in public. It was a symbol, but it was not *only* a symbol.

When Jesus invited his disciples to the Last Supper, he first washed their feet, freed their feet, liberated them, unbound them from the most crippling bondage of all—not the bondage of being dominated, but the bondage of being domineering. "So if I, your Lord and Teacher, have washed your feet, you also ought to wash one another's feet."

What we celebrate here is a great unbinding, two great unbindings. On the cross Jesus unbound the bonds of sin that had bound us head to foot, hand to heart—free at last, free at last. And at the same time and in the same place and by the same means Jesus unbound us from the bondage of binding others, their feet, their hands, their mouths, their minds—free to serve, free to serve.

God, for the grace of having been liberated we give you thanks. And for the grace of liberating others we give you thanks, through Jesus, Amen.

WITH ALL THE SAINTS

I pray that you, being rooted and established in love,
may have power, together with all the saints,
to grasp how wide and long and high and deep is
the love of Christ and to know this love that surpasses
knowledge—that you may be filled to the measure
of all the fullness of God. (Ephesians 3:17-19)

Although our culture celebrates All Hallows Eve, we
have the opportunity to celebrate All Saints Day, a day for
all saints to commemorate the contributions of all saints.
Paul prayed that we "have the power to comprehend, with
all the saints, what is the breadth and length and height
and depth." But the breadth and length and height and
depth of what?

The words bring to mind the cross of Christ, with its
horizontal and vertical beams, its multi-dimensional mercy.
Spanish artist Salvadore Dali's painting of the crucifixion
shows Christ hanging on a huge three-dimensional cross,
hanging across the sky, representing the immeasurable
riches of his grace.

But another work of art may depict the breadth and
length and height and depth even better. It is an ancient
crucifix, a carving of Christ hanging on the cross. But the
cross itself has disappeared, been removed or rotted away.
All that is left is Christ, reaching one pierced palm to his

crucifiers, one rusty-nailed wrist to the co-crucified. His gaping mouth cries to the heavens for forgiveness for those gathered at his feet. His feet are crisscrossed and crushed.

There is a wideness in God's mercy, a largeness to his love, as wide as the ever-reaching arms of Christ, as high as that horrible head, as deep as the ruddy roots of his love. And that love is a love that reaches all the saints, all the saints with whom we recognize the far-reaching effects of the cross. So it is that we gather to recognize the broad, long, high, deep love of Christ. And when we gather at this table we also recognize the broad, long, high, deep body of Christ, the community of the saved, the saints—all the saints—for whom he died.

God, we pray that our love for the saints might be as broad and as long and as high and as deep as your love for us in Christ, Amen.

WITH WHAT WE HAVE

**You see, at just the right time, when we were
still powerless, Christ died for the ungodly. . . .
God demonstrates his own love for us in this:
While we were still sinners, Christ died for us.**
(Romans 5:6, 8)

Olivier Messiaen was already a well-regarded church
organist and composer when Germany invaded France
in 1939. He volunteered to serve as a hospital attendant,
but soon found himself with 20,000 other Frenchmen in a
prisoner-of-war camp in Poland. Conditions were harsh,
but Messiaen continued to compose on smuggled staff
paper and an old piano. He also discovered three other
musicians who managed to bring their instruments—a
clarinet, a violin, a cello with only three strings. Under
those difficult circumstances and with that odd assortment
of instruments he composed one of the century's finest
pieces of classical music—*Quartet for the End of Time*. It
celebrates the immortality of Jesus Christ. Five thousand
prisoners gathered on a frigid January day for the
premiere, the most attentive audience, Messiaen observed
later, he ever had.

We come with what we have. Some gather at this table
under difficult circumstances—pain, conflict, turmoil.
Some are prisoners of forces inside and outside. Many have

limited resources, like musicians with no instrument. But here we are, with what we have, doing what we must. Here we are, with what we have, even though the conditions at work, at home, in the world, maybe even at church, are harsh, continuing to celebrate the life and death and life of Jesus Christ. Here we are, with what we have, from different backgrounds, with different needs, but sharing the imprisonment of sin and the longing for true liberty. Here we are, with what we have, horrified by what the past has brought, fearful of what the future might bring, continuing to celebrate Jesus.

May the clink of each cup and the crunch of each piece of bread in the meal we are about to eat be like a great ensemble of praise to God, no matter what our limitations, no matter what our circumstances, because we have come with what we have.

God, here we are, with what we have. Use us as instruments of your praise, through Jesus, Amen.

ZERO DEGREES LONGITUDE

Let us run with perseverance the race marked out for us. Let us fix our eyes on Jesus, the author and perfecter of our faith, who for the joy set before him endured the cross, scorning its shame, and sat down at the right hand of the throne of God. (Hebrews 12:1, 2)

It is no work of art, not even a wonder of technology—the odd, ornate observatory on top of the hill in Greenwich, England. It sits a few miles down the Thames from busy, bustling London, this quiet unassuming spot that is in some senses the center of the world.

It is the earthly, earthy reality underlying the artificial line that suddenly leaps from under your finger on the globes of your spinning youth, this inauspicious spot on the unlined face of the earth in Greenwich, England.

Zero degrees longitude.

It has a lot in common with where we stand this day in this place, this here-and-now. This table where we gather is no work of art, no wonder of technology. We, the people who gather here, are no work of art, no wonder at all. And these simple acts at this plain place are somewhat less than we might expect, less grand, less miraculous, as we repeat this earthly, earthy, odd, old act. But gathering at this place makes us more—more somehow centered, more secure about starting, starting over, starting out, on our journey, on ourselves, for having stood around this table, the Lord's table, our zero degrees longitude.

For this is where we start, at the foot of this table, at the foot of the cross, the place where his life came to an end and our lives began, begin, begin again, again and again, begin over, over and over. It may not seem all that impressive at first—this place, these people, these actions—like Greenwich. But like Greenwich, this is where we mark the beginning of time and place, the table of the Lord, the Lord's Supper, zero degrees longitude.

God, we pray that you give us the courage to begin anew every time we end up at this our starting point, through Jesus, Amen.

SCRIPTURAL INDEX

Genesis 3:6	*First Meal, Last Meal*	39
1 Chronicles 16:1-4	*First Thanksgiving*	43
Song of Songs 2:11-13	*The Feast of Regeneration*	37
Isaiah 53:5	*The Bloody Crucifix*	17
61:1	*Binding the Broken*	15
Malachi 4:2	*Greeting the Rising Son*	47
Matthew 20:26-28	*Her Own Share*	53
26:26-28	*All the Broken Pieces*	9
	First Meal, Last Meal	39
	Not Just Words	73
Mark 6:48-51	*A Monsoon Meal*	67
8:34	*Marching with the Cross*	63
10:45	*Slave to the Slaves*	83
14:15	*Another Upper Room*	11
Luke 2:34, 35	*Christmas Needs Communion*	21
15:32	*Standing Up Together*	89
22:14	*The Longest Table*	5
22:15-21	*In the Presence of His Enemies*	57
	Judas' Eyes, Jesus' Eyes	59
22:19, 20	*The First Meal on the Moon*	41
	Something's Fishy	85
22:25-27	*Everyone is Equal*	33
23:34	*Father, Forgive*	35
23:44, 46	*Grain and Grapes*	45
24:30-35	*Encountering Christ*	31
John 1:14	*The King of the Hawaiians*	61
2:1,11	*In Our Gladness*	55
3:16, 17	*Traveling by Starlight*	99
6:11	*Something's Fishy*	85
8:11	*Drawing in the Dust*	27
10:11	*The Shepherd Wears a Crown*	81
12:32	*Bringing in the Cross*	19
13:3-5	*Dirty Feet*	25
	The Emperor's Table	29
15:13	*A Monument to Love*	69
16:33	*A Place of Peace*	77
21:13	*Something's Fishy*	85
Acts 5:30	*Hanging on a Tree*	49

Romans 5:6,8	With What We Have	105
6:4	Thunder at the River	95
12:1	Strapped to the Cross	91
12:5	A Part of the Whole	75
1 Corinthians 11:23-24, 26	He Broke It	51
	They Still Ate	93
	Thunder at the River	95
2 Corinthians 5:21	Digging His Grave	23
Galatians 5:1,13	Unbinding Their Feet	101
Ephesians 2:15-19	The Saddest Place in the World	79
	Speaking His Language	87
3:18, 19	With All the Saints	103
Philippians 1:20, 21	Michelangelo's Masterpiece	65
Hebrews 4:14,16	At His Footstool Kneeling	13
10:5,7,10	Tokens of Triumph	97
10:11, 12, 14	All the Blood is His	7
12:1, 2	Zero Degrees Longitude	107
Revelation 5:9	The King of the Hawaiians	61

TOPICAL INDEX

Aldrin, Buzz	The First Meal on the Moon	41
All Saint's Day	With All the Saints	103
Angelou, Maya	Standing Up Together	89
Art	Drawing in the Dust	27
	First Meal, Last Meal	39
	Grain and Grapes	45
	Judas' Eyes, Jesus' Eyes	59
	Michelangelo's Masterpiece	65
	The Shepherd Wears a Crown	81
	Something's Fishy	85
	Strapped to the Cross	91
Baptism	Thunder at the River	95
Beginning	Zero Degrees Longitude	107
Christmas	Christmas Needs Communion	21
	They Still Ate	93
	Traveling by Starlight	99
Cross	Binding the Broken	15
	The Bloody Crucifix	17

	Bringing in the Cross	19
	Grain and Grapes	45
	Hanging on a Tree	49
	Marching with the Cross	63
	Tokens of Triumph	97
	With All the Saints	103
Cyril	*The Feast of Regeneration*	37
Death	*Another Upper Room*	11
Dream of the Rood	*Tokens of Triumph*	97
Equality	*Everyone Is Equal*	33
Family	*The Longest Table*	5
	A Part of the Whole	75
Fiction	*Digging His Grave*	23
	Encountering Christ	31
	In Our Gladness	55
Film	*Binding the Broken*	15
Forgiveness	*Father, Forgive*	35
	First Meal, Last Meal	39
Franz Joseph, Emperor	*The Emperor's Table*	29
Good Friday	*The Emperor's Table*	29
Grace	*Christmas Needs Communion*	21
	The First Meal on the Moon	41
He Qi	*First Meal, Last Meal*	39
Holan, Vladimir	*All the Broken Pieces*	9
Humanity of Jesus	*The King of the Hawaiians*	61
Humility	*At His Footstool Kneeling*	13
	Dirty Feet	25
	The Emperor's Table	29
	Everyone Is Equal	33
Hunger	*All the Broken Pieces*	9
Ignatius	*Traveling by Starlight*	99
Journey	*Traveling by Starlight*	99
Joy	*In Our Gladness*	55
King, Martin Luther	*Another Upper Room*	11
Koyama, Kosuke	*He Broke It*	51
Lazarus	*Michelangelo's Masterpiece*	65
Love	*A Monument to Love*	69
Magnus	*Father, Forgive*	35
	A Place of Peace	77

Mercy	*With All the Saints*	103
Messiaen, Olivier	*With What We Have*	105
Morning	*Greeting the Rising Son*	47
Music	*With What We Have*	105
Oe, Kenzaburo	*Digging His Grave*	23
Origen	*Dirty Feet*	25
Outcasts	*Drawing in the Dust*	27
Plymouth Colony	*First Thanksgiving*	43
Poetry	*All the Broken Pieces*	9
	At His Footstool Kneeling	13
	Tokens of Triumph	97
Polycarp	*In the Presence of His Enemies*	57
Repentance	*Judas' Eyes, Jesus' Eyes*	59
Resurrection	*The Feast of Regeneration*	37
	Greeting the Rising Son	47
Reynek, Bohuslav	*Grain and Grapes*	45
Rinza, Shiina	*Encountering Christ*	31
Sacrifice, Service	*All the Blood Is His*	7
	Digging His Grave	23
	Her Own Share	53
	In the Presence of His Enemies	57
Slavery	*The Saddest Place in the World*	79
	Slave to the Slaves	83
	Standing Up Together	89
Spring	*The Feast of Regeneration*	37
Storms	*A Monsoon Meal*	67
	Thunder at the River	95
Suffering	*Marching with the Cross*	63
	The Saddest Place in the World	79
	They Still Ate	93
	Unbinding Their Feet	101
	With What We Have	105
Taj Mahal	*A Monument to Love*	69
	A Part of the Whole	75
Thanksgiving	*The Longest Table*	5
	First Thanksgiving	43
Wedding at Cana	*In Our Gladness*	55
Woden	*Hanging on a Tree*	49